WITHDRAWN

D1482947

How **Muscles and Bones** Hold You Up

A Book About Models

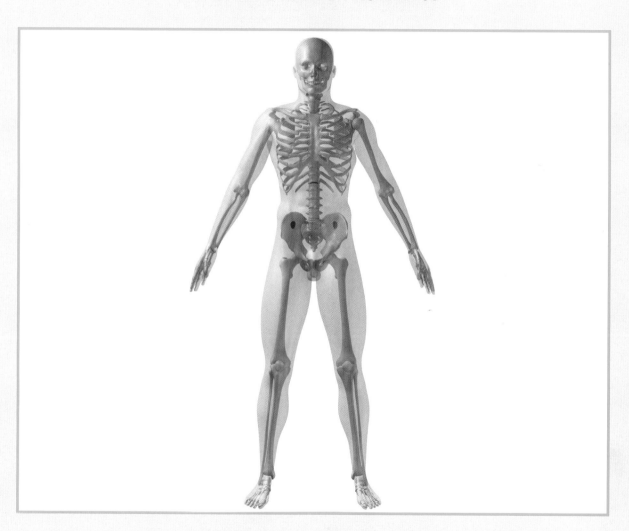

Marcia S. Freeman

Rourke

Publishing LLC
Vero Beach, Florida 32964

www.rourkepublishing.com

PHOTO CREDITS: Title Page: © Sebastian Kaulitzki; Page 4: © Elaine Davis; Page 5: © Paulaphoto; Page 6: © Linda Bucklin; Page 7: © Patrick Hermans; Page 8: © Philip Date; Page 9: © Sebastian Kaulitzki; Page 10: © Sebastian Kaulitzki; Page 11: © Kanwarjit Singh Boparai, Sonja Foos; Page 12: © Sebastian Kaulitzki; Page 13: © John Lumb; Page 14: © Galina Barskaya; Page 15: © Patrick Hermans; Page 16: © Costing Cojocavu; Page 18: © Peter G; Page 19: © Leah-Anne Thompson; Page 20: © Renee Brady; Page 21: © Renee Brady; Page 22: © Hashim Pudiyapura

Editor: Robert Stengard-Olliges

Cover design by Michelle Moore.

Library of Congress Cataloging-in-Publication Data

Freeman, Marcia S. (Marcia Sheehan), 1937-
 How muscles and bones hold you up : a book about models / Marcia S. Freeman.
   p. cm. -- (Big ideas for young scientists)
 ISBN 978-1-60044-539-2 (Hardcover)
 ISBN 978-1-60044-700-6 (Softcover)
 1. Musculoskeletal system--Juvenile literature. I. Title.
 QP301.F73 2008
 612.7--dc22
                                2007018236

Printed in the USA

CG/CG

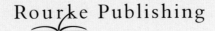

Rourke Publishing

www.rourkepublishing.com – rourke@rourkepublishing.com
Post Office Box 3328, Vero Beach, FL 32964

Table of Contents

Our Skeleton

Have you ever seen the wooden framework of a house? Our body has a framework, too. It is made of bones.

But unlike a wooden frame, our bones are not nailed or bolted together. Ligaments, muscles, and tendons hold our bones together.

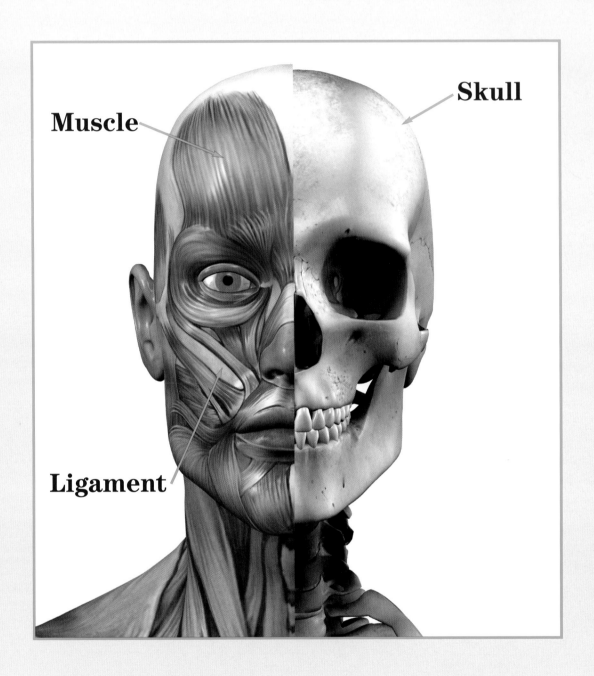

Muscle

Skull

Ligament

Ligaments attach one bone to another. Ligaments are like pieces of stiff elastic that can stretch a little when the bones move.

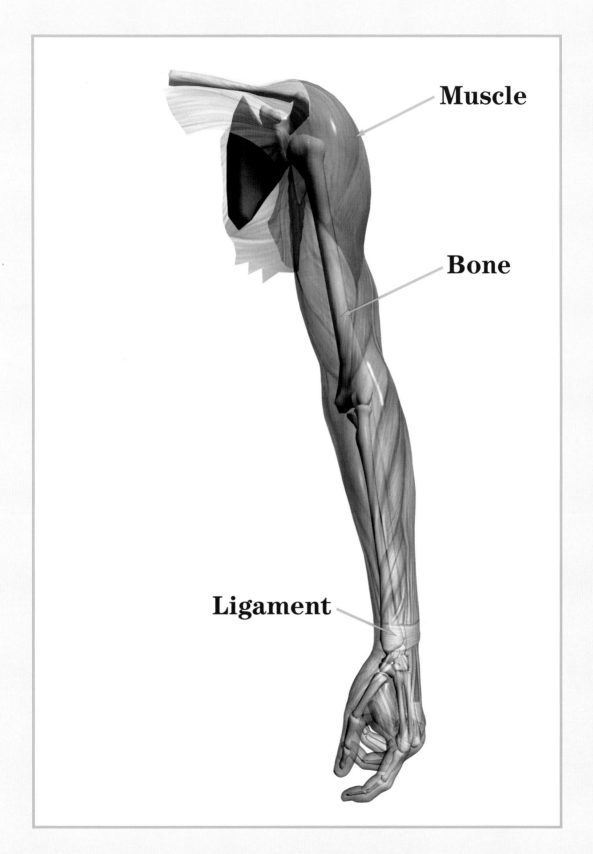

Muscle

Bone

Ligament

A Replica Model

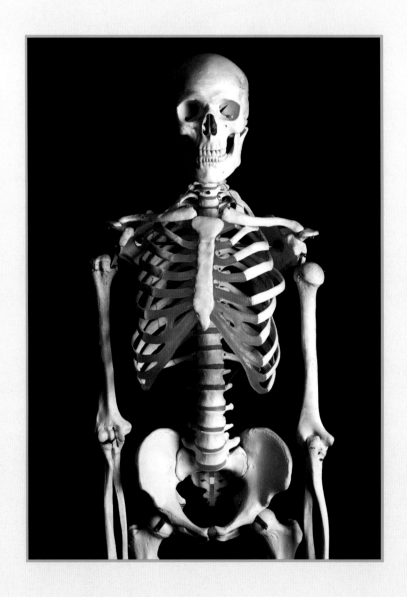

How can we learn what our bones, muscles, tendons, and ligaments look like and do? One way is to study a model. A model represents things that are difficult to see or measure.

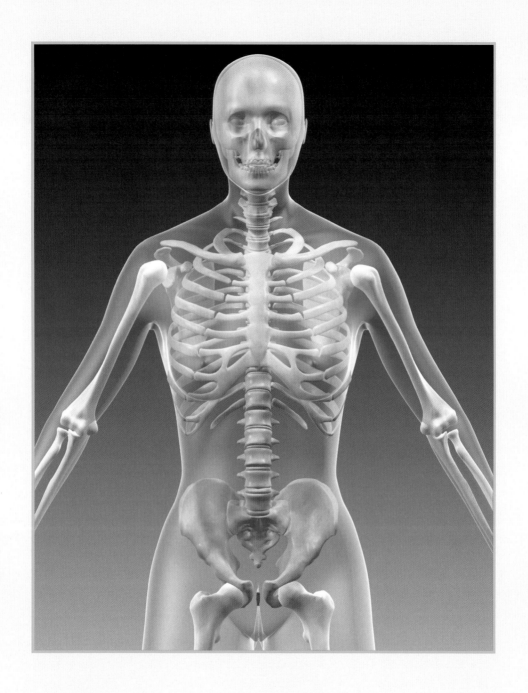

A plastic model of our skeleton shows how our bones are arranged. It is a **replica** of our framework.

Joints

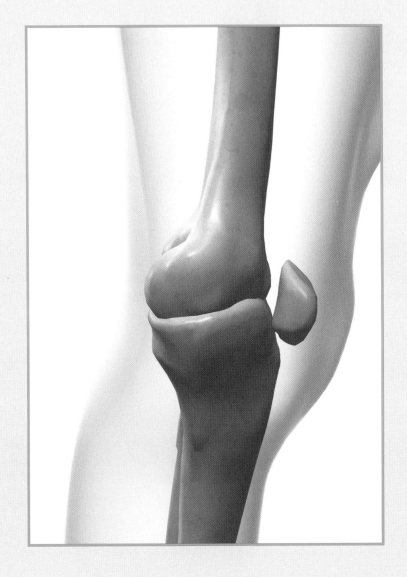

Bones are connected at joints. Some joints are like door **hinges**.

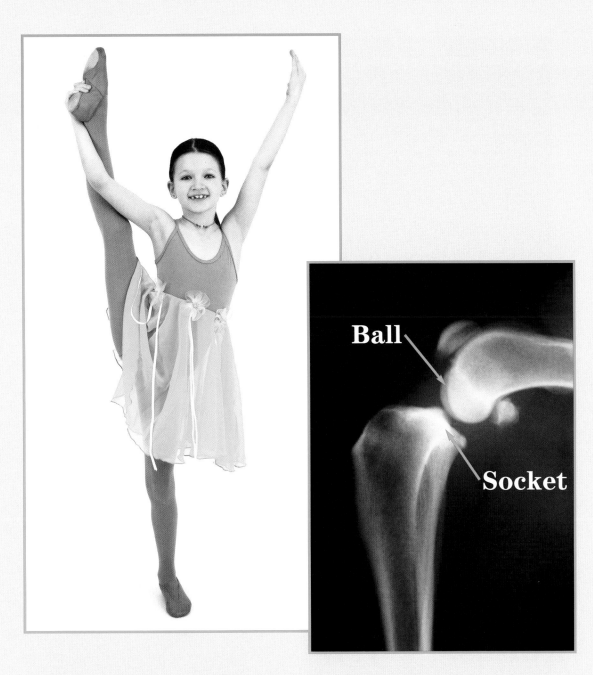

Ball

Socket

Some joints have a ball and **socket** arrangement. Ball and socket joints let us move our legs and arms forward and back, or in a big circle.

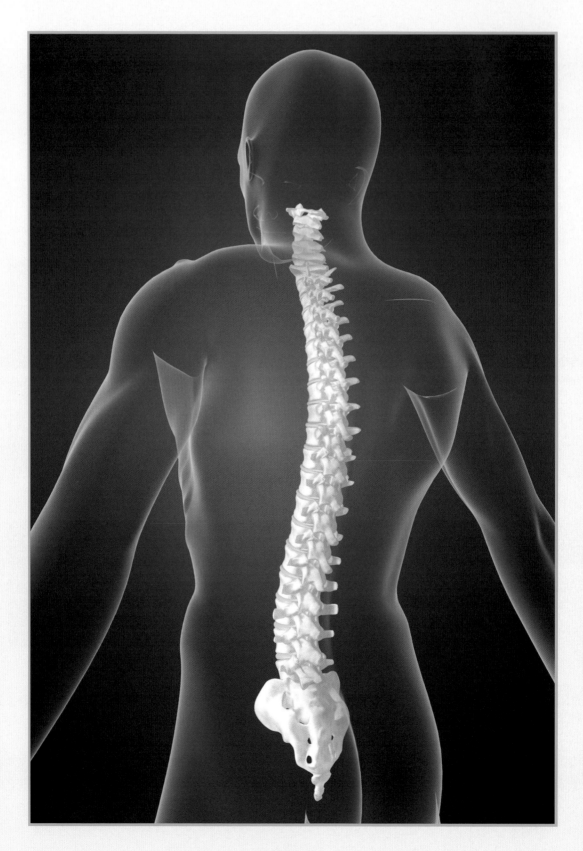

The bones in our back—the vertebrae—
are stacked with a soft cushion-like disc
between each bone. This arrangement lets
us twist and bend.

Muscles and Tendons
Let Us Move

Ligaments hold our bones together, but muscles make our bones move.

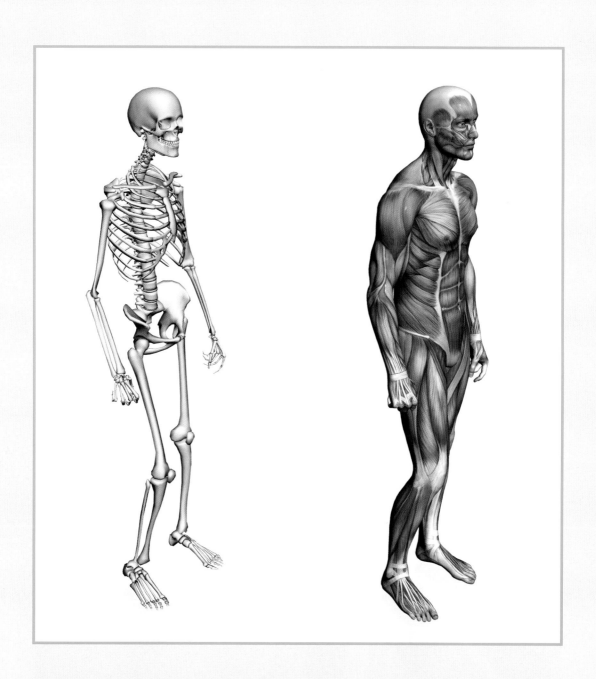

Without the work of our muscles we would be just a pile of bones in a bag of skin.

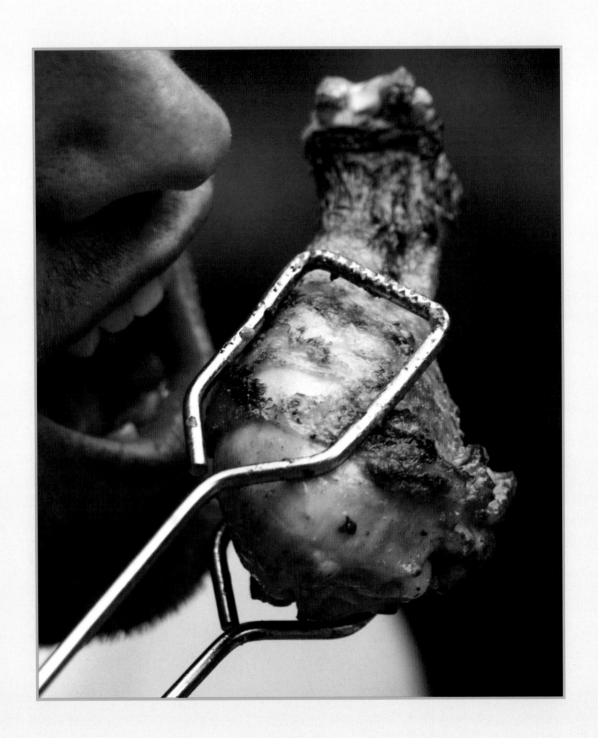

Muscles are attached to our bones by tendons. If you eat a chicken leg, you can see tendons and muscles.

Notice how the leg muscle—the meat—ends in a whitish rubbery band. That is the tendon that attaches the leg muscle to the leg bone.

A Representative Model

How do muscles move our bones? We can construct a model to show how our muscles and bones work together.

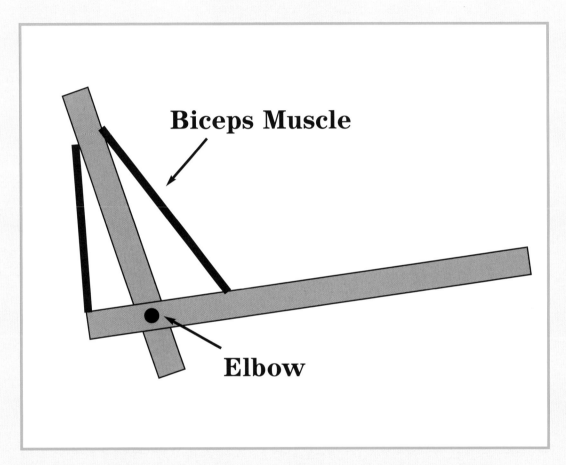

This model of an elbow shows how our arm bends. It shows how we can lift something. It is a representational model.

Squeezing a balloon represents what
happens when you contract (flex) your
biceps muscle.

Now relax your arm and notice what happens to your muscle.

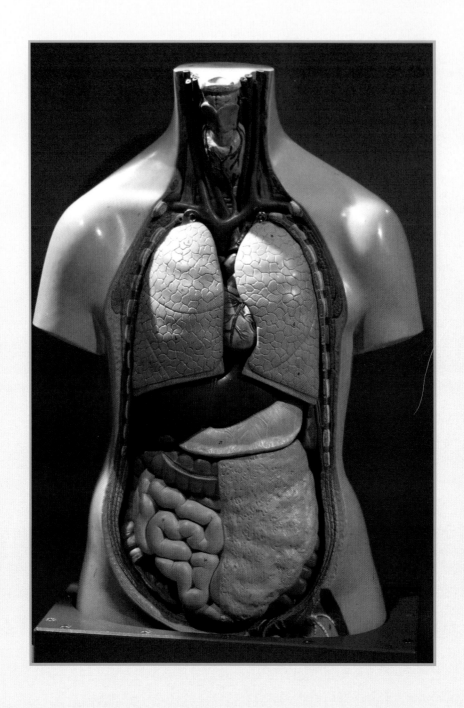

Models help us figure out what things look like and how things work.

Glossary

biceps (BY ceps) — one of the main muscles of the upper arm

disc (disk) — a flat, round object

hinges (hinjz) — jointed or flexible devices that allow the turning of a part, such as a door or lid

socket (SOK it) — a hollow into which a part fits

replica (REP le kuh) — a copy or reproduction

Index

Further Reading

Seuling, Barbara. *From Hand to Toe*. Holiday House, 2002.
Arnold, Caroline. *The Skeletal System*. Lerner Publications, 2005.
Johnson, Rebecca L. *The Muscular System*. Lerner Publications, 2005.

Websites to Visit

www.rad.washington.edu/radanat/elbow
www.surfnetkids.com/human.htm
kidshealth.org/kid/ill_injure/aches/broken_bones.html

About the Author

Marcia S. Freeman loves writing nonfiction for children. Her fifty or more children's books include science, geography, and math titles. A Cornell University graduate, she has taught science and writing to children and their teachers from kindergarten through high school.